I Wish I Had a Heart

Like Yours, Walt Whitman

I Wish I Had a Heart Like Yours, Walt Whitman

Jude Nutter

University of Notre Dame Press
Notre Dame, Indiana

Published by the University of Notre Dame Press
Notre Dame, Indiana 46556
www.undpress.nd.edu
All Rights Reserved

Reprinted in 2012

Manufactured in the United States of America

Library of Congress Cataloging-in-Publication Data
Nutter, Jude.
I wish I had a heart like yours, Walt Whitman / Jude Nutter.
p.   cm.
ISBN-13: 978-0-268-03663-8 (pbk. : alk. paper)
ISBN-10: 0-268-03663-2 (pbk. : alk. paper)
1. Violence—Poetry.   2. Violence—Philosophy—Poetry.
3. Suffering—Poetry.   4. Aggressive behavior in animals—Poetry.
5. Human beings—Animal nature—Poetry.   6. Political atrocities—
Poetry.   7. Anti-war poetry, American.   I. Title.
PS3614.U884I3   2009
811'.6—dc22

2008051314

∞ *The paper in this book meets the guidelines for permanence and
durability of the Committee on Production Guidelines for Book Longevity of
the Council on Library Resources.*

FOR MY FAMILY,

and in memory of PETER ROESCH JAMES

Snatches of speech on the airwaves: *help us.*

In such times only hurried notes,

moving to no conclusion, a fool's work

to make anything of them, a liar's to make nothing.

— Ken Smith

Contents

Acknowledgments

Grateful acknowledgment is made to the following journals in which these poems, or earlier versions of them, first appeared:

Chautauqua Literary Journal: "Growing up in Bergen-Belsen: Sleeping with Anne Frank," "*Espenbaum* in Bergen-Belsen, May 2007," "Road Kill"

Great River Review: "In the World Museum"

MARGIE: The American Journal of Poetry: "The Helmet," "Triptych for My Father," "Dinner in the Suburbs," "Growing up in Bergen-Belsen: The First Kiss"

Nimrod International Journal: "Growing up in Bergen-Belsen," "Triptych with Birds"

Notre Dame Review: "The Centrefold," "The Lover"

Sycamore Review: "Goats"

The Missouri Review: "Growing up in Bergen-Belsen: The Chrysalis," "How to Use a Field Guide," "The Insect Collector's Demise"

The Southern Review: "Lamb"

Tor House Newsletter: "Four Girls"

Wilderness: "Wolves"

Winning Writers (online): "For Those Held Captive for Decades in Darkness," "The Map," "Infidelity," "Selling Honey on the Road to Sarajevo," "Untitled," "Love and the Hangman in Croatia," "*Via Negativa*," "Visiting Uncle Peter's Grave," "Carolina Grasshoppers"

"Goats" was awarded the 2007 Wabash Prize in Poetry from the *Sycamore Review*.

"For Those Held Captive for Decades in Darkness," "The Map," and "Infidelity" won the 2005 War Poetry Contest sponsored by Winning Writers of Massachusetts. "*Via Negativa*," "Visiting Uncle Peter's

Grave," and "Carolina Grasshoppers" took third place in the 2008 War Poetry Contest.

"Growing up in Bergen-Belsen: The Chrysalis," "How to Use a Field Guide," and "The Insect Collector's Demise" were awarded the 2007 Editors' Prize from *The Missouri Review*.

"Growing up in Bergen-Belsen: Sleeping with Anne Frank," "Road Kill," and "*Espenbaum* in Bergen-Belsen, May 2007" were part of a submission that was awarded the 2008 Poetry Prize from the *Chautauqua Literary Journal*.

"Triptych with Birds" was part of a submission that took second place in the 2008 Pablo Neruda Prize for Poetry from the *Nimrod International Journal*.

I Wish I Had a Heart

Like Yours, Walt Whitman

LAMB

Saw a new creature's first moments of thinking.
Felt the chill blowing through me.
— Michael Dennis Browne

I thought she was resting with her head against the fence
until I saw the wire, exact as a grass blade, pressed
against her open eye. Ravens will loot a body quickly
for its softest parts. She was newly dead; she was clean,
storm-washed. At the keyholes of the nostrils, those flies
the colour of ochre that follow the flocks all summer
and lay their eggs upon the shit in the fields.
I've watched ewes and lambs finding one another on the hillsides—
calling and answering and moving, always, toward the sound.
Her lamb in the field now on the pins of its legs, its tail
like a whisk, its mad rattle unanswered, bolting
from ewe to ewe and each ewe, in turn, lowering her head,
hooking it under the belly, lifting and pitching it away. Not mine.
Not mine. Not mine. Saw it looking around at the hills.
Saw it turning in circles. Saw myself standing back,
doing nothing. I took the track up and out
of the valley to where the wind devoured
the lamb's monologue of panic; until the tragedy unpacking below
became part of the view—a detail in the story, not the whole story;
until the dead sheep was a white bag held against the fence
by the wind, and the lamb a pale mote floating about the field.
The lake, the burnished water, a man with a black dog
in the reeds lining the river, gunshots, and ducks spitting skyward
like flung gravel. Even from a distance, suffering
is suffering. There was wind breasting through the surface
water of the lake; there was crisp grass with green light
up its sleeves. There must have been sunlight but it was shadows
I noticed, small hauntings in the hills as the clouds slid past.

THE HELMET

Under the wind's cold roof we are lost and homeless,
And the flesh is flesh . . .

— Loren Eiseley

You have been lying so long with your face
against the earth that the dirt beneath your cheek
is warm and your teeth have a coating of grit
and dust. In your body, a great heaviness.
As if you had swallowed your own grave. So
it's true: a man can eat a shallow depression
in the dirt to get his head just below
a sniper's line of fire. Hour after hour the artillery
and the mortars coax dark mouths to open
in the duff and the muck, and there are times
when a man—photos, long bones, muscles, hardware—opens
with them. While fifty yards away,
where the light is whole and the trees unbroken,
you can see the wind's white shoulders moving
through the unspoiled grasses.
And how many times in the life you had
before this one, did you cross, without thinking,
walking upright and whistling, a distance
of fifty yards? When the man right beside you dies,
you know it, without looking: at the heart
of the barrage, beneath the cough of mortars,
enveloped in flame and slaughter, you feel,
far off, on the inside of your body,
a new loneliness. First
there is nothing more than his great stillness;
then, around his head in the dirt, the long-
furled banner of his blood appearing. Under

the skull's curve, inside
the heavy meat of the brain, the rooms
of his mind, their doors blown open, stand empty.
You notice his hair, darkened with sweat,
a fold of skin above the collar of his battle dress;
how sunlight is thrust like a dowel
through the tidy stigma the bullet has punched
in his helmet, which has come to rest beside you,
now, on the battlefield. Alive or not,
each man here is equally dead; and so, in a lull
behind a screen of smoke, you put on
his helmet, aware that a helmet pierced by a bullet
will help you, until danger has passed or darkness
falls, in feigning death. And so the mind begins to rehearse
its own oblivion.

Long before he knocks off the helmet to press
the narrow rictus of the Luger against your temple,
you smell the breath of the barrel. He is your age—
no more than twenty—and his eyes are ransacked, empty,
the windows of a mansion gutted by fire. But after holding
your gaze for the briefest moment, he steps back

and holsters his pistol; and flat in the dirt,
in a fever of grief and fatigue, you are no longer sure
if he is real, or a dream with a heart made kind
by carnage and darkness, or even which possibility
you might prefer. Either way, after holding your gaze
for the briefest moment, he stepped back
and holstered his pistol. Either way, he has passed you over.

IN THE WORLD MUSEUM

WORLD WAR I DISPLAY

. . . and over here, drones the docent, *a collection*
of smaller, more personal battlefield items. His tour
group are boys so it's trench dioramas they want, and tanks
and shell casings tall as they are; and so

as they pose and measure up against the tracks
of a rusty Whippet, I make my way to the glass display case
in which someone with a taste for irony has arrayed,
as if setting a place for some formal dinner, a complete set of silver,

non-regulation cutlery dug from the mud of Gully Ravine.
Instead of a plate there is the shallow, upturned bowl
of a British helmet, positioned, I suppose, so we can look inside
to see how metal peels, petal-like, back

from a bullet hole and is as thin as paper which is something
an Austrian soldier marooned at the front did not have
because placed like a serviette on the right is a postcard
of tree bark addressed to the brothers Stickling

in Vienna. Birch, I think—you can see the dark flecking like runs
of stitching in the bark, and still, after all this time, that distant,
non-committal sheen like the demeanour of moonlight on water;
and suspended at eye level on a strand of monofilament

is a single boot. French. Size 8. Small, really, for a soldier.
Still tightly and evenly laced and because of this
one detail alone, almost beautiful. The real promise of art
is that it might rescue us from the literal. A helmet. Place settings

of silver. A postcard of birch bark. A single boot. To each,
a different story. But to each story, the same ending.

ANGLO-SAXON DISPLAY

In the case before me the blades of a *seax* and a sword;
the flared, black knuckle of an axe head. Men,
it seems, slept, and were buried, with their weapons.

And anyone who's ever loved a soldier knows
that when he is sleeping the hands of such a man
are like the shuttered paws of the lion—more terrible
because he is sleeping. Even the crafty,

clever lighting, even suspending each weapon
inside its own soft hammock of brightness, can't separate
its form from its function. How easily we grow tired
of the obvious. But the meanings of the objects found

with the bones of women remain ambiguous: boxes
holding scraps of fabric, spheres of crystal and amulets
carved from the joints of sheep; false keys thought to symbolize
availability and high status. Ambiguity itself is a form of seduction:

look, these are keys to the gates of possibility and myth. And look:
without the glaze of the imagination, the world is

what it is. Notice how the heads of the spears
were long and slender and so took advantage
of the joins and the gaps in a man's armour.

Imagine if everything the Buddha claimed is true and all
things external are illusions. But who wants a world,
illusion or not, in which a witness can sit all day
on the banks of the Kagera watching bodies

from the war in Rwanda coming over the falls
and then later describe how they never once appeared
to be really dead: *they looked,* he said, *like swimmers*
because strong currents invested them with the power

of movement. The past might be over
but it's never done with. *Leave them in peace,*
said Stalin of his favourite scientists who were lost
in projects important to the state; *we can kill them*

later. History: a ledger of atrocities. Remember
those who never ceased trying
to undermine the rhetoric of governments: Goya
at the end of his life—deaf and lonely but still

bearing witness, painting directly onto the walls
of his country house outside Madrid. It is said
that after Goya there were no more innocent rifles in art,
no more sticks uttering puffs of smoke and fire. Remember

Ed Murrow, live from Buchenwald after liberation.
For most of it, he said, *I have no words.* For most of it.

Not all of it. Murder, he said, rags and remnants.
I looked out, he said, *over the mass of men to the green*
fields beyond. A ledger of atrocities. Another hostage, another
smart bomb gone astray in the market; collateral

damage and acceptable losses and somewhere one more child
dead before it can be named; and for millions, home
the place they are homesick for, even as they live there.

Here and there, the ragings of art: a ledger of atrocities. History.

Untitled

Still to come: what's growing in your microwave a special Eye-
witness Health Report you can't afford to miss and one of the first
Ukrainian soldiers to arrive at Auschwitz-Birkenau and now living
in New Jersey tells us what he remembers of that historic moment
sixty years ago today plus a new rapid procedure that dramatically
reduces wrinkles you have to see it to believe it all this and more.
After the break . . .

— local newscast, 27 January 2005

So it continues: the marriage of tragedy
and the banal. The news anchor wants a story
but all he is given are fragments, scraps
and mouthfuls of memory. *Teeth. Each one full of silence.*
Where? How many? *Beyond counting.* In thirty days
we can all look ten years younger, wrinkles and worry lines
melting away. *Hair, tons of hair. Shoes and toothbrushes.*
How many? *Beyond counting. Whine of light on the wire;*
clothes piled up like the pelts of animals. There are microbes
thriving in all our microwaves. *And bodies, corpses. Don't ask*
how many. In the Kommandant's garden the loose,
worked earth of the flower bed; an ornamental cherry
shattered by gunfire. He's tired, distraught, not
a good subject. All the anchor wants are a few slick stories, easy
Hollywood chronologies, but all he's getting are fragments,
scraps, small mouthfuls of memory. More

than enough. Fragments are the story; without them
there can be no story. *On the wall, stigmata*
of bullet holes beyond counting. The effort it takes
to keep the heart's gates open to history and its heavy cargo.
There is no other work. Once, and years ago,

hitching alone from Prince Rupert to catch
the eastbound Amtrak train from Seattle, I remember
the regular swathe and smudge of wipers;
the husband, in the front seat, tilted
and twisted strangely toward the window, holding
his wife's right hand. His silence, which I took
for indifference. She and I talking about writing
and the weather: small bursts of language then long
periods of green blur and drizzle. In Lakeview,
stopping for petrol; watching her husband stutter
across the forecourt; understanding, only then,
that the way his torso twisted and tilted him forward
from the waist was permanent. Him
coming back, then, to the car; stretching his arm
out to hand me water and a bar of chocolate
and, as he did so, the loose cuff of his shirt
slipping back so I saw there the string of faded numbers
in the skin of his forearm. *Auschwitz,* he said,

as if clearing his throat. *Birkenau,*
he said, holding out the water so our fingers
touched. *I was ten. Bags of cement and gravel.*
They broke my spine. For you, he said, and his fingers

relaxed as he released and I accepted
his gift. I'd got it all wrong—
his silence, I mean—because what possible use
would any of us have, later, for language,
if the narrative of the life we had when we were ten
had been reason enough to kill us. He never spoke
his name. And how does it end?
It doesn't. Evening. The train station
in Seattle. A fine rain still falling. Watching them

pull away from the curb and into traffic. Waving.
And I've been saying it since to everyone I know
and it's been slipping beneath the skin
of every poem I write and how does it end? It doesn't.
Repeat after me: *Auschwitz-Birkenau. A boy. The beautiful
new ladder of his spine. Broken. Bags of gravel
and cement.* Don't ever tell me this isn't a story.

GROWING UP IN BERGEN-BELSEN

1

We all grow up among the dead.
But for a child, I had so many. In fifteen minutes—
less time than it took to kill hundreds—I could ride
my white, three-speed bicycle, out
through the front gate, over the cricket pitch, down
past the pig farm and into Bergen-Belsen.
The house I grew up in appears on a postcard mailed
by soldiers of the Wehrmacht to their families
sometime during their training
in nineteen thirty-nine; contained, toward the end
of the war, eight hundred sixty-nine Gypsies,
Jews, and others—overflow from the camp
next door as Stalin advanced and Hitler
panicked and prisoners were shuffled west.

2

The year I began to grow breasts, my body,
once private and belonging to me
alone, began to belong to others. This was the year
boys began to smell strange, like objects
that never dried out, like the rank
hug of air in the bunker at the end of the street
with its odour of concrete and its gun
slits flush with the ground; the moist neck
of the stairwell in summer. Twenty-five years
since the end of the war and still we had dreams

of finding soldiers in full battle dress with every
single bone intact; with their helmets and pistols
and bayonets. This was the year my body
ran away with itself and I
spoke less and less, while even the thoughts
of the boys I ran with began to sweat
as they signed up for that life-long apprenticeship
to their wet dreams. I had no knowledge
of the soul, but what I did know was ruinous
and simple: that the body was punishment
enough; and so, as revenge
for their every snub and humiliation, this
was the year I began to draw my teachers
naked, limbs akimbo, floating
on the white, unlined pages of my school notebooks.

3

We invent ways to live with the body.
And then it is taken away. I grew terrified
of touching the pictures of the sick and the dying
in *National Geographic*s and Sunday supplements,
washing my hands over and over, opening
doors with my elbows, or not at all.
It wasn't guilt: the guilt of children is local—shame
over someone else's Cat's-Eye or an Aggie
dropped into a pocket as it dribbled out of bounds;
an apple lobbed on a dare
through the school bus window;
the countless insects starved by mistake,
year after year, locked in jars
with parts of the green world they could not eat.

4

Then came the year I stopped eating, convinced
that appetite itself was murderous. *You quickly
discover,* said a camp survivor,
that you will kill your own child for a crust of bread.

5

The white mare injured in the pasture,
who lay in the grass on her side and ran,
like a dog in dreams, on the growing
blanket of her bleeding; the tadpoles I collected
who chewed the tails of the weakest among them
down to tatters; a rabbit, clipped
by the car in front, flopping in the gutter
as we roared past awash in smoke and grit.
How could I not believe that our sufferings
came back to the fact of the body. Roil
of minnows in a hand net. The frantic
epilepsy of pale, thin bodies
like the sound of distant clapping. Despite
what you might have heard, the birds do sing
in Bergen-Belsen. They sit in the trees, fat wallets
of song. And I grew up with other, common
myths: lampshades and handbags of human skin;
hair of the murdered made into wigs for the whores
of the SS guards. And myths are terrible
in the way they worry upward, in layers, like bones
or pearls, around kernels of truth and hurt: one
small event, a single word—it's this brush with the truth
that gives them their terror. And their power.
And this was how I came to language,
with such fear in my small body. And it would burn
down through me like a wick.

HERON

The green wires of the lily stems
gradually vanish, dropping away to their anchorage
in the lake's back pocket; but they have given
permission for their leaves to flounce
upon the water like a field of spread skirts, and I
am sliding through them now inside
the pod of a silver canoe, the varnished paddle
rising, then falling, as the evening moves
forward out of the trees and small fish arrive
at the surface with their hunger, each mouth
a noose closing and opening around nothing.
It's a miracle any of us survive.
Think of John Clare in his poverty writing his poetry
on thin slates of bark; who, through his madness,
found a way of surviving. Think: twenty years
in the asylum; food, good boots, and a place to sleep.
All the paper he would ever need. I should be happy

there are no barriers against such need
and passion. How he took the things he loved
and locked them away behind the barricades of language.
How he knew that surviving
simply meant keeping the things he loved from harm.
How he lived there with them. Even though
the things he loved
were the most dangerous things of all. How
    in faith, the great
    blue heron lobs the weight of its body forward,
    ahead of itself, over the water, dips and then gathers
    into itself.

FOR THOSE HELD CAPTIVE FOR DECADES IN DARKNESS

What if you had the job of erasing, filling in, and covering over the
names of the missing as the missing were found and identified?
Surely you could claim you raised the dead for a living?

— journal entry after visiting the Monument
to the Missing of the Somme at Thiepval

For those held captive for decades in darkness
I rise in darkness and take up
the tools and utensils of my trade—the trowels
and tiny, flexible palette knives for pressing
cement and mortar deep into the hairpin curves
of letters, into the arches and alcoves of a name.
A name is a word and a word, after all,
has an ambience. Like a room or a building. I bring
the dead forth out of exile, one
letter at a time. *Ah,* wrote Whitman, *the dead to me mar not . . .*
they fit very well in the landscape under the trees and grass,
and along the edge of the sky in the horizon's far margin.
Well, I wish I had a heart like yours,
Walt Whitman, but I earn my keep in a country
where the bones of boys and men have been walking
for close to a century now through the soil.

Most will walk downward forever and never be found.

And with so many bones in its mouth the dirt
will never stop singing. And the living
to whom such bones belong must rise
every morning exhausted and homeless, alive
but lacking a plot of earth beside which they might fall
on their knees and weep; but one remnant, one fragment—

a tag, a ring, the sod-stained, abandoned chancel
of a skull with a few teeth anchored, still, in the sling
of its jaw bone—is enough: the earth
is our temple and our grave and a heart won't rest
until its dead have tethered it in one place.
It's a miracle that a man can trickle
down to where earthworms rummage
through the earth's dark flour, vanish
into the cauldron of his own dead mouth
and spit back, decades later, his own bones and buttons;
that a man can amount to less than a handful
of trinkets sifted from the dirt's top drawer.
And when you come here it is best to forget
the tourists, and the students with their worksheets
and notebooks; best to pick a single name
and carry it inside you all day and remember
how this was a man once—a tall column of flesh—
how his name must have fluttered
all through childhood like a pennant
about his mother's lips; and how later,
as a man's name, and if he were lucky,
it was taken and held for ransom
inside the willing mouths of different women.
One name. Any name. Any one name
out of seventy-three thousand. I take my time. I erase

him letter by letter until he is a whole man, a complete
body—not a man of war, not a warrior, but a man labouring
under nothing more difficult than his own desire,
who lay down in a field and fell asleep
beside a woman he loves; the woman he turns
to and reaches out for, the woman who is fastening
the buttons on the bodice of her dress as she rises, laughing,

out of the warm grass, the sky at her back like god
in his firm, blue helmet. It doesn't matter how
we call the loved one, the lost one, the golem
up from the earth, or that our icons are breath and dirt.
Such are the roots of worship. *Lay down*

your silence, I say. *Take up your name.*

GROWING UP IN BERGEN-BELSEN:
THE CHRYSALIS

This is not war . . . this is timeless and the whole world and all
mankind are involved in it. This touches me and I am responsible.
— Alan Moorhead, journalist, Bergen-Belsen,
24 April 1945

We all grow up among the dead.
But for a child, I had so many.
In fifteen minutes—less time than it took
to kill hundreds—I could ride
my white, three-speed bicycle,
out through the front gate,
over the cricket pitch,
down past the pig farm
and into Bergen-Belsen. The house

I grew up in appears on a postcard
mailed by soldiers of the Wehrmacht
to their families sometime
during their training in nineteen
thirty-nine; contained, toward
the end of the war, eight hundred
sixty-nine Gypsies, Jews, and others—
overflow from the camp next door

as Stalin advanced and Hitler
panicked and prisoners
were shuffled west. And this past
chose me, and I acquired my destiny
and the shadow of that destiny
followed me everywhere, and this
is how I became possessed

by the memory of some task
I had yet to do. The butterfly,

remember, must haunt the body
of its first self, hidden deeply there,
and in a different form. And this
is what it means to be burdened
by the future and it must
mean everything to dream yourself wings, wake,
and pour into your life.

I don't remember how or when
I saw my first photographs
of Bergen-Belsen; of bodies
being pushed and rooted forward
and piling up against the broad-
bladed grin of an army 'dozer;
of prisoners on their knees among stacks
of bodies, on their knees and preparing
a meal of turnips. Bodies

like netted leaves on the wire
and so much light as if the sky
had simply lowered
its forehead to hold them
there. To speak of the world
in terms of something else
is a habit of survival. Say it:

those were human beings
caught up on the wire.
And left hanging on the wire.
And so much sky. Say it:
this touched me

and I am responsible.
This was the year of my greatest
discovery: the barbed
and buffed lime-green locket
of a peacock butterfly tethered,
still, to its stem and lifted,
carefully, out of the nettles.
It was the only evidence I had
of a magic so real it felt like a dream.
Imagine being able to break
down the body you have
and rebuild it, then, into something better.

And if I could vanish into myself
and come back into this world,
I would want some evidence of welcome,
I would want to rupture back
toward a light that's familiar,
and this is why I packed that jar
with twigs, and bruised leaves,
and grasses. And this
was my undoing. Overnight

that butterfly emerged and became
caught up in such a world and when
I woke it was a slender failure

between the collapsed tents of its wings.
How is it we can rupture so hard
toward a future while the world

for which we burn has other plans.
After this, my jars stood empty

because I could not undo
that wound, and I could not undo history,
the house into which I was born,
or the fact that I had stood, quiet
and still, on the very ground
across which human beings
had been bulldozed into pits. I

cannot change the fact that a poem
is a gesture of welcome, and why
would I want to, because for those
of you who have vanished
into yourselves, this is how
you come back, now, into the world:
here it is.

THE CALVES

in the pasture accept everything
that does not harm them: varnish of rain
on the wire and wind
wrapping then unwrapping its quick gifts in the grass
as the storms pass over; the lung
of a plastic shopping bag deep in the hedge;
even the burning that descends and then assembles
among them into the flame of an egret,
its beak's stiletto the hue of ripe lemons; and yet
no matter how often I walk the road in silence
to lean against the cold scaffold of the gate, they balk
and scatter to a rubble of shapes against the distant
boundary of the field. Somehow, in memory,
are the shadows of those who will come to hurt them,
with their sticks and their bolt guns,
with their boots and fists. So, the impala inherits the lion;
and the minnow the pike's lean slipper and any
shadow that falls onto the platter of the water, and some
inherit more than others: the frog, for example,
on the tongue of the lily, rich with hints and panic.
Survival is secular, protein and ash, and life,
it seems, loves itself enough to hand even us
snippets of memory: loose dogs, blind curves
and sinews of rope; storm drains, culverts, the rifle's
clean throat. Hidden motives and small bones
in the plush-green gutter of a ditch. I have closed
all the curtains and every door.
Around me, in the house, all things tidy
and each thing in its place so I'll know
what the world is up to when the mind—

common moth at the heart's uncurtained window—
turns to its work and the body slips free
of its moorings, all patience and dust. I write:

> *The calves in the pasture accept everything*
> *that does not harm them.* Even their own,
> fresh bodies, which they slowly inhabit,
> which will, at some point, turn against them.
> Which contain no malice.

Triptych for My Father

Night Patrol, January 1945

Because they have a need to pray
with more than their knees against the earth,
they are prostrate in the garden

of the bombed-out farmhouse, with the damp wicking up
through the small thickness of their khakis. Aftertaste
of shellfire and blood and the cold

barrels of their rifles. And such peace: from deep
within the house they can hear
the slow trickle of powdered plaster. Then, my father's

voice—soft thread on which each young heart is strung—
whispering the order and the whispered order passing
from one man to another, in darkness:

move forward. Think how each man has to place his mouth
against the ear of the man right beside him. Imagine
the sudden, hot bloom of breath; here and there a pair of lips

pressing, by mistake, against a cheekbone
or a neck. The yearning, and regret, this kindles.

Xanten, March 1945

The morning you were wounded, Churchill was there—
well rested, wearing clean clothes—motoring
up a hill with Montgomery's aide to oversee the opening
and first hours of battle. It is always a question

of perspective: what is war to a man on a hilltop at dawn
with a layer of good soap on his skin
and clean clothes? I have no perspective. Just imagination.
I imagine you falling, arms flailing, legs scythed

from beneath you by Spandau fire, the phlegmy churn
of small bullets entering the water. Then the sharp,
steam odour of your own, opened body. Mud and gristle.
What is war to a man splayed wounded on his back

in the dirt of Germany, his stomach full of hard tack
and Compo tea; while above him, like the deep
inner lining of a dream he has misplaced, hangs
the pale fascia of the sky's calm curve. *Forward,*

wrote Churchill, *on wings of flame to final victory;*
and that night, high-spirited, full of port and German pheasant,
he read aloud, for Montgomery's amusement,
from Maeterlinck's *Life of the Bee*—a book of anecdotes

and frivolous dalliances. While around him
the dark, packed hive of Europe smouldered and seethed.

RESURRECTION

The death that haunts you most now
you never witnessed—Grant, the big-boned Scotsman,
after less than an hour on his first patrol, blown
to offal on a bridge. But you talk still

of his forty-minute war and how the bits of him that floated
like torn fabric on the water come together
almost nightly in your dreams until he rises
inviolate, a whole man, from the flaming currents

of the river and comes forward through the flak
and the barrage. This is how the work
of resurrection is done—by the living,
every night, daily, over and over: think of Isis

gathering together the scattered, severed pieces
of Osiris in no other world but the world
of her own imagination; of how a painter
works and reworks a canvas until there is something alive

between the bone and the final varnish.

Via Negativa

in memory of my uncle, Peter Roesch James, Mosquito VI navigator and gunner, 45 Squadron RAF. Killed in Burma, 28 February 1945.

1

The way a sudden break in a song
makes the song more apparent.

I came to know you only
as the things you were not.

Not a single tooth, said my mother; *not a button.*
Not a button, not a tooth, not a bolt, not a bootlace.

Not a goggle lens, a dial glass, a whisper
of oil. *Not a single slug of rubber.*

Not even a rumour of fuselage or bone.
We each came to believe

the story we needed to believe,
and this is how it was that we let you die

several different deaths at once even though
you were given only one.

2

The official report on your death arrived—the details
assuaging, perhaps, the need for a body. Sometimes,

when the living can endure their losses no longer, words
can do this: sometimes
words stand in for the world.

You are not light walking the curve of your own spillage;
you are not foliage, not smoke, not flame,
not a green so complete it tasted vicious.

Not static on the wireless, cutting out. Not vomit
or blood or the dive
your pilot could not pull out of. You

are not even the sound of your own voice crying out.
Not even the loss of that sound.

Not the gutter of your own throat
flushed with rain. You are only an absence

obligating me to make certain
that the life I have
be enough. And the hope

I have carried, always, is for some last thing
of which I am not yet aware, through which you
will at last step forward. Because

what use am I to you, little god of negatives,
if you will not finally appear? It is time.

3

October. Among the robins flocking in the marsh
it seems there is always one who insists on breaking
into the stashed, bone box of his spring repertoire

to sing in protest against his own departure.
Even when his song is lost
behind the static of a world intercepted by rain,

it is there. I feel it. Long, braided
straps of song. It is time.

4

There was a lover.
And you were thinking of her and her
white dress. Of her and her white dress.
Of her white dress and the parachute
you didn't have the height or the time
to use; of her white dress as it lifted
and filled and held you

against the drop. There was a lover.
And she always remembered you
as that one, unrepeatable moment when
getting dressed once after love
the light, efficient and sophisticated, licked
up the short run of your fly
as the teeth of its zipper locked back together.

GOATS

The trick is to make memory a blessing . . .
— Dana Gioia

Down on your knees, you sift through the past
with your father; when he leans in you catch the aftermath
of his shampoo and evergreen shower gel and, beneath that,

the deep, familiar combustion of the body—the room
in which we sleep, each one of us, every night of our lives
with the windows closed. Here's a picture of you in Denmark—

around you, torsos of trees like the long-polished bodies
of brass instruments. How happy you were. And what a shock
to realize you no longer remember what such happiness felt like.

And here you are at that gypsy fair in Cyprus where you
and your father ate cold sweet corn, sold on the cob
from wicker baskets filled with ice, while, among the rocks

of the walls, scorpions slept on in drawers
of shadow with, now and then, a wink of armour as sunlight
returned to the world's great room as the clouds

went over, and you wandered, by accident, into that agon
under the almonds where the young goats were being slaughtered
for the spit. Dust and a few pale shocks of grass. How weightless

they appeared; how swiftly each was hoisted and strung
from the branch by its back legs. Shackle of fingers around
each muzzle. Each throat angled for the knife. Your father

remembers dropping his hands to the yoke of your narrow
shoulders, wheeling around and steering you, like a bicycle,
down the hillside and into the crowd; but the things

he believes he spared you are not the things
that have come to haunt you. Yes, you tell him, you remember
the quick scarves of blood, the plump torsos twisting

and pitching, how the front legs galloped as the body struggled
to keep ahead of what it knew was coming; the tree branch
bouncing wildly and blood on the ground skinning over

in the heat and fresh pips of blood sending up blown kisses
of dust. Then the stillness that settled, the lax
stretch of the body, and the head, nearly severed, swinging,

a scarlet bell, level with the butcher's crotch.
How the smoothness of an animal peeled out of its skin
is familiar and terrible, the glint of its nakedness

almost human. But what haunts you is the memory
of those lying trussed in the shade, waiting their turn; the soft,
clogged sounds of their language and how they never once

stopped talking, quietly, amongst themselves; the almonds
in the trees, each one locked in its golden suitcase
among the leaves, and the leaves like the polished tongues

of church shoes. All these years your father has lived
believing he saved you, which is every father's wish
and failure; and you don't know what to do, now,

to assuage his sadness other than promise yourself
you will write about this even though art is like the past
and what we learn to love is a fiction, and what we come to trust

might never have existed, and what we remember
never really happened the way we remember it. The way
they strained to reach the sparse grasses and every leaf,

shaken loose, that came down within reach; how,
until the last permissible moment, they took the world in, small
mouthful by small mouthful and, right there—

where the lion-yellow mouths of sunlight dropped
through the canopy and opened up in the dust—
turned it over, slowly, between their teeth.

SELLING HONEY ON THE ROAD TO SARAJEVO

POTOČARI, NEAR SREBRENICA, 2005

Groundsheets of mist.
The sweating of grasses.
It covers the boots of the workers
breaking the earth in their windcheaters
and bright anoraks.
It eats the blades of their shovels.

Down on their knees
among them are the women, opening
the soil up with their hands.
They might as well be digging their own graves.

The clucking of stones like worry beads.
Hands and the blades of shovels like plates
presenting the dirt; everything
they have left, which is almost nothing.
Gusts of grief and longing.

Hair torn loose from a headscarf.
Red fruit for the workers. And coffee. And row after row
of graves, each one the length of a body even though
all that might be left is a tiny tray of bones

or, more often than not, much less than that.

> *The woman holding part of a shoe with a thread*
> *hanging from it. The shoe of her son,*
> *which she had mended. The woman sobbing*
> *over a single rib. The woman who recognizes*

the teeth of her husband. And begins to kiss them.
The woman who has nothing but the memory
of making love, blinding herself
to the fact that their country had gone to war
since they last bought groceries. The woman
who has nothing. The woman who has less
than nothing.
The woman sitting quietly beside a tiny cairn of bones
who says: "Please, let me touch him just once more."

LOOK NO FURTHER

It doesn't matter how little we are given—
watches, belt buckles, splinters of bone. Imagine
the discipline it must take to recognize,
when they have spent years in the ground, the teeth

of someone you love. It should
make us grateful to know it is possible
to love with such attention. Imagine the safe,
banked taste of the soil; even the ghost of the body long
gone now inside the earth's dark bag.

We could hide behind metaphor.
But what use is metaphor when it makes emptiness
less than it was? All we need is a woman
kissing the teeth of her dead husband. We should look no further.

I have quarreled with my god. I will have nothing
to do with him. He is perfectly impossible.
An image I keep bearing: a wounded child
hidden by a newspaper in Pavelić Street;

the paper's headlines, words of violence,
details of curfews. We bought flowers and the war
engulfed all names and religions. It was
but a small step, then, to the edge of town
where we were cut down like beasts. War
is always unfinished business:
I never found the words for a life
split in two. Bosnia, hope and dream, a mad
house, a battered suitcase thrown to the ground
during a bloody halt on the long journey.

THE LONG JOURNEY

Spent bullets and piss and cigarettes
on the floor of the sniper's nest. Mines and borders
in the hills, the fur of an animal caught low on the wire.

Convoys of supplies held up in the mountains.
The child who knew enough to keep silent
among the spent bullets and piss and cigarettes.

Fact: men fight for what they believe
without knowing what it is they fight for.
In the hills, the fur of an animal caught low on the wire.

There were graves dug nightly in the city parks.
There were pop cans that soon became hand grenades.
There were spent bullets, there was piss, there were cigarettes.

But in every war there are miracles and stories of luck:
a stray donkey grazing its way through the minefield,
in the hills, the fur of an animal caught low on the wire.

The lies dealt out by the state: forget them. Remember
the things you've never been told but know, even so, to be true.
Spent bullets and piss and cigarettes.
In the hills, the fur of an animal caught low on the wire.

> *He was murdered. There was no grave.*
> *There was a quest that became an obsession*
> *leading to shards and fragments, a dim sense*
> *of terror. Bones*
> *roaming through the streets of the burning city until*
> *everything that moved was finally*
> *silenced. But something escaped*
> *and overcame the pages deleted from history.*
> *The quest is arduous. It began*
> *and it will end in a small room, in boxes of papers—*
> *notebooks, letters, diaries—in which you might well find*
> *some pictures of your father. Bow to the evidence.*
> *It contains, like a shadow, the essence*
> *of what is sought. To everything—*
> *to the river, to the poplars and willows, to the silent*
> *ravens on the highest branches—a firm foothold.*
> *And to you: believe you will die in a better world.*

AFTER THE PARTY

You can't begin to know what it feels like, he said,
unless you've been there. It's impossible to describe, he said,
I can't find the words for it.
As if these facts alone are reason enough to stop trying.

As if to remain silent in the face of atrocity is not
a political act. And how, if he can't find words for it, can he know

what it really feels like? And how, if we can't find the words
for the sufferings of others, can we claim
to speak for ourselves? And what does it feel like,
really, to be part of a war you cannot escape from?

He had his passport, his press card, his ticket over
the border. His avenue of exit. Whiskey
and slivovitz in the safe zone. *Shoes,* he said,
so many shoes, in the streets
by the river up in the hills. Imagine running so fast you lose
your shoes. Imagine having your shoes taken from you.
Imagine someone, a neighbour, moving in close
and sneering: *You won't need shoes where you're going.*

And years later, when it's over, the networks
will airily announce that refugees are returning and cleaning
up their country, as if they had merely stumbled, slipped
off the pavement and spilled the groceries; as if
they were hoovering the apartment after a party. Oh

look, a leather jacket forgotten in the bedroom! Oh look,
a red sling-back behind the stereo! Oh, look how all
that can be salvaged of our father, missing for years,
will fit into a single shoe.

> *I went. Like many others. I came away*
> *with what would not leave me.*
> *I reached beyond the grimace of suffering,*
> *the blood that was shed, into the gut*
> *of our dying century. I believe in the story*
> *I want to tell. The intimate betrayals*
> *of myth and legend, the lurid*
> *power of past violence. History as prison.*
> *The carnage. The secrets. The last families*
> *scattered and broken, mirrors of their country.*

Genocide. Cowardice. The failure of policy.
The strange, unwieldy attempts to palliate
damage. How hopeless and ridiculous
are borders drawn in blood.
I heard words steeped long in love
and friendship. But they grew rarer and rarer.
Overwhelming: bodies among the ruins.
Suitcases. Books. Scraps of clothing. Unthinkable
that we should know so little of the wounds,
the bereavement and division.

THESE DAYS

War, convenient and visible.
Faithful, the voice of despair.
The utter folly of shaping a country
that could not be found. An angel
extricated us from our dreams
at random. At random,
the singular, cold executions: friends,
braver than was reasonable, cut through.
In them live the mysteries, for which
I thank them. The journey began:
in darkness for years we lived,
a war between us. And the pursuit
of peace? The light
that sustains me? That takes longer,
is more painful, the hardest road.

There were grants to rebuild mosques and churches, grants
to start strawberry farming, beekeeping, bakeries,
grants to rebuild houses. Whenever
I wonder how it's even possible
to return with nothing

to a country that cannot be found, I remember
there are women selling honey,
now, and strawberries, on the road to Sarajevo
and most of what they need is close at hand: the gentle,
productive Carniolan honeybee, and the mountains, the herb-
covered mountains, the gardens and wild mushrooms;

narrow alleys of the old towns, ramshackled beauty
and the glimmer of water, men with cigarettes in the shade
of the trees. The shade of the trees
a second dusk.

ESPENBAUM IN BERGEN-BELSEN, MAY 2007

for Paul Celan

Espenbaum, dein Laub blickt weiss ins Dunkel.
And only language could ever
set me down, here, in daylight,
inside such a darkness.
Whistle of sunlight like bird bones in the heather

as I stand alone on the newly-opened
main road into the camp. Before me
this slender silver birch, pulled up
by the workers, which someone has stripped
of its bark, wreathed in wire
and planted back

into the earth with its roots in air. And your poem
has bled a little into the wood—each word,
now, with its taproots of black ink. I think
of the thousands who passed, here

and elsewhere. A mile away, on the ranges,
the 7th Armoured are on manoeuvres—the thick,
rolling yammer of machine guns and in my chest
concussions of artillery like missed breaths.
Closer in, the small, resonant rooms

of the cuckoo's two-step; and, closer yet,
in a gauze of sunlight under the trees,
two young Germans, stripped
to the waist and on their knees, working
with the chime of trowels against gravel,
with laughter and whistling and the soft

fret of the glottal stop. If such work
weighs them down they refuse to show it even though
they have already laid bare Block Nine's
foundations, and, in the woods behind, the long,

slim gut of a pit latrine and a sty in which the SS
fattened their pigs. That a stranger would furl
your words about the torso of a tree. That your words
would become their own mouth. You worked so hard—
your whole life—toward this, I need to believe
such a moment would have saved you.
Think of the dead: cinder, splinter and ash; ashes,

ashes, bone and button. Each tooth's thimble,
a name; each name a throat filled with shadow;
and, from this, leaves rising up
from the earth's deep clinker.
I think of the dead but glance

toward the living, who are beautiful and oblivious
to their beauty, stripped to the waist
and on their knees wearing gloves of dirt, and I
will forgive myself but will not
apologize because this is what the dead do:
make us restless and eager, sharpen
our hunger, urge us to offer

our bodies up into the mouths of others.
And we might believe language

is our one, true refuge, but see how easily
the world retreats behind its closed lips: throat,
thimble, earth's deep clinker.

I pulled down the roof
above us, you wrote, *slate by slate,*
syllable by syllable. Because

there is no refuge: the mass graves
of Bergen-Belsen will always be graves. And the dark
will flex its mouths forever against the graves
and the leaves of the aspen in equal measure.

FRAGMENTS

(Aftertaste of the heart's
green running. Each leaf, each flower, each blade
a turbine. Yes,
each leaf opens into its gifting; the fingers
of the lily are already dressed
in colours they have carried
all along. All soundless
burning and the waiting for death. Remember,

without words we remember nothing.
Language condemns us, one
memory at a time, to a world we can,
or cannot, live with: This body,
or that body? That lover or this lover
above all others? This flower
with the wind in its cowl, or that one?
This road at dusk? Or that road?
That bullet or this bayonet? This night of torture
or that night? This death? Or that one?
We each have our own war. As if one
is not enough.)

You were following orders:
he had a weapon,
was pulling it out of his pocket.

                              I was still moving toward him
                              but I was on my knees, which had blown
                                        inside out, like flowers.
You sensed hostile movement in the trees.
                    There were birds moving through the trees,
                        their agitation more specific than the wind
                                        and deeper in.

I saw a flare of sunlight on the sight of a rifle.
I simply discharged my weapon.
Your whole head became a slick mouth.
No, I don't dream about any of it.
You are afraid to sleep in case you dream
and remember things you didn't know you'd seen.
I went back to what was left
of my house. In the courtyard
I found my donkey, half dead
and braying in the ruins, wearing stockings
of blood and shit.
There were days you ingested terror.
But whose terror you never could tell.
Yes, I gave the orders: I was following orders.

There were no trees left: imagine, a city
with no trees. I dug up graves
and broke up coffins
for burning.
The dead
under moonlight
under wind.

The dead
under moonlight
under wind.

I was on my back in the ruins
at the bottom of the sky's blue chimney.
Even when you dream your heart changes
in a way you cannot describe.

Bodies
jockeyed from the rubble, I dragged
them into the new world. A world in which
those who could have named them
no longer lived.

The bullet casings fell so fast
for so long it began to sound like singing.
Despite the gunfire, my child in her crib, sleeping.
You told yourself so often you had nothing
to lose so when you finally lost everything
you wouldn't even notice.
Between hammers of gunfire, a garden gate, creaking.

(If we are ever told: *you have no right to speak*
because you've never been there,
we must ask: *is there anyone among us, dead*
or living, who was born into a world without war?)

You discovered a suture in the human heart,
a tiny bridge. It will take decades to cross.
On one side there is damage. And on the other,

damage.
My dead did not live long enough, or,
if they did, I was not listening.

I tasted blood. It wasn't mine.
I was fucking *breathing* it in.
You watched soldiers collecting the corpses:
saw how they shot them first, making sure
they weren't packed with explosives.

You saw the pigeons coming home.
You watched them circle for days.
You saw them die of heartbreak and watched them drop,
exhausted, onto the ruins of their roost.
Before the war your heart did not ache.

                                    I think of my dead parents. I pray
                           that when they dream they never dream
                 they are mortal, or, if they do, that they wake with relief.
Your memories will not behave.
There are so many words and yet not one
that is terrible enough. You talk
all the time and hear only
your own silence.

                    I lost count of how many times each one
             of them took the handles of my new-sprung pelvis
      into his hands and tilted it to his liking. But my flesh remembers
                              every single angle.
Even now when sleeping a part of your heart
keeps vigil on its own behalf.

                      I swear the women became fit
             and beautiful: it was their way of fighting a war.

                    I stopped painting the things I witnessed
           to write poems instead. Just because I could hide
               them in the hollowed-out heels of my shoes.
            I walked for months on my own words. I knew
if you were killed that your poems, having carried
you for so long and coming to their own conclusions,
would simply go on walking without you. (Yes,

         each leaf opens
         into its gifting. Each leaf, each flower, each blade
         a turbine. Aftertaste of the heart's green running.
         All soundless burning. And the waiting for death.
         The soul's prison? Or the body's prison? This death?

Or this one? This prison. This death. This life:
these longings
that are our lives: these fires

                    going out in the grass. *This life,*
    this life, this life: these words
    before all others.)

RAVEN

The way Jesus drapes across the thighs of Mary,
his arms, in death, stretched wide, reminds
me of a raven I once lifted up by the hammock
I had made of its wings. Ants busy already

on the dark avenues of its feathers. In order
that it would not be taken and lost in the world
forever, I spread it flat on the roof of the woodshed,
where wind and rain made its demise feel cleaner:

death, fresh from the shower, all sharpened
edges and correct grammar. Months later,
in a bowl with a chipped rim, I washed
away the final argument and song of the flesh until

all was bone, white as the teeth of beauty queens;
and under the bill sheath, which slipped
off cleanly like a high, black boot, the beak's
pale taper. I love how the Lord's long body

is, at last, unequivocal; how everything that's mortal
about him is wholly obvious now, now
that he's finally a man, dead, in his mother's arms.

Triptych with Birds

for my mother

I

It will rain, and all night it will rain, and the waters
will run so dark with tannin for days that the rivers
will not slip free of their slick, black boots. And she

will be adrift in the glass-bottomed boat
of delirium and be, by dawn, beyond reach
even though I will have slept the whole night beside her.

Look, she will say, *I can see straight down
and into what I knew would happen: my body,
so hungry to live, eating itself.* I know

the logic of fever is like the logic of a dream
and that the body's appetite can sabotage
what it loves best, and I will begin

to dream of mouths where no mouths should be.
The storm will clear and all afternoon
the clouds will move loosely over and the wind

will chase its pennants through the grass and sunlight
test its tongue along the hedge backs, polishing
the coinage of the leaves so they shine

like the worn soles of shoes. So much burning
without flame. What matters is not
what I'll remember, but how I'll remember it: not

that her breathing will be difficult, but that it will be
almost secret, like the first bird waking—no singing,
yet, but a delicate stirring in the leaves of the escallonia;

not that the first bird will arrive at the feeder,
but that a bullfinch will arrive and cling
to the slim basket of seeds, his waistcoat on fire.

2

I am up at first light, crows
passing over,
a run of snips in the sky's blanched awning,

the world's black lining; on the lawn,
two doves in matching collars
of pewter, and a solitary

robin, that beguiling blaze of his chest
an invitation, like a man unbuttoning
his shirt in public

one button too far. Rain on the helmets
and throat guards of the stonechats' dark armour.
Amid the fuss there is always one, grounded

by damage, in the grass: a chaffinch,
his left foot crushed and twisted,
who cannot get a toehold on the thin wire mesh

of the feeder. Every morning I find him, gleaning
what the rest in their enthusiasm
let go—whole seeds, crumbles of suet—

and what I feel is more than relief.
It is a kind of gratitude. And so late in my life.
My mother sleeps on, well past noon,

and her sleeping feels like a separate life.
I am alone. I have not been abandoned. I watch
that bird and the way his wings close,

perfectly, against his body
like envelopes being sealed; how he waits,
without fuss or fanfare, and misses nothing.

3

Out in the bay, a small boat, its rubber skin
glistening like a seal's. Three small figures in scarlet
life jackets. The blue clarity

of deep water. Blue. *Azul.* A shadow
is bluest when the body casting it has already
vanished. I sit with her, inside those pockets

of radiance that open up within a storm,
and *who's there* she cries, startling
awake each time the room becomes wild

with a sudden yawn of light and I
feel it too: a door opening
directly from this world and, for a moment,

it is everywhere—blue of pressed breath, blue
like a taste of history; the fascia-like glare
on the spine of a book forced open

too far and a body
to which similar things are happening. Afterburn
of a struck match. There are no blues

in the caves of Lascaux.
The masks of the Incas were blue. A hawk
glides in, low, over the garden, and the birds

at the feeder in their panic rise up
as the crucifix of its shadow passes
over the grass. And so death

has slipped into the poem. On the colour wheel,
blue is closest to white. Out in the bay
the small boat slides behind the curtain

of the sun's late glare on the water.
I am thinking of Giotto's Saint Francis
talking to the birds, how the birds

stutter down against the blue's
high-minded backdrop; how he painted in
a few extra so that he could simply

wipe them, deliberately, from the canvas; how
their shadows remain, like a dream
of a memory about birds. And I

understand, now, what he's saying: that there
was a body here, then it was leaving. Then gone.

VISITING UNCLE PETER'S GRAVE

The map is crude and difficult
to decipher; but slowly—plot by plot,
row by row—I make my way
along the cemetery's slim green corridors.
I could find you easily enough, now,
without the loupe, but I need
you to appear in the way you always
appear: a letter and two numbers in a magnified
circle of print; the rough edges of your grave's
drawn boundaries a mild crumble
of dirt along a fresh-dug ditch.
Where you lie buried with your pilot.
Your death twin. Your darling.
When they found you I suppose your body
and his had everything in common.
There are many such graves
at Taukkyan and I have coloured
the map green because we forget, we forget
that the grass is one long breath. And each week
I pencil a flower onto the small, worn
tray of the page. It is early November.
West, and just beyond

the cemetery's walls, are the Thamin
and the barking deer of Hlawaga Park
and, twenty miles south, well off the page, Rangoon
in its grey hammock of rivers. Your grave is a lie
created for the living, because what more
would you have been but a sachet of ash
tucked down in the soil? In the war footage of planes
going down the smoke, literally,

blossoms. Like water; like the chambers water
builds in the frit of its turning
at the base of a fall; then a last, lazy
rain of debris and dirt. We forget, we forget
there is death at the heart of it. In the crucible
of the cockpit you achieved, without choice
and without effort, what every lover strives for,
and yet, not even lovers know what it means
when a body refuses to declare itself

and fall away from another's. And yet
the long tongue of one river simply slides
into the throat of another, and a man can lift
his shadow from the ground and still have it be
his shadow. West, and just beyond

the cemetery's walls, are the Thamin
and the barking deer of Hlawaga Park
and, twenty miles south, well off the page, Rangoon
in its grey hammock of rivers. Where it is,
already, tomorrow. Peter, even wrestled
to a standstill in the dirt, you cross every threshold
before me. And I do nothing but place flowers
down in your wake. And, when it is finished,
I will steal lines from the mouth of this poem

and abandon them
in the cemetery's slim green corridors.
And whatever I leave will be evidence,
the marks of a flourish toward permanence.
And whatever I leave will never perish
to make room for anything else.

GROWING UP IN BERGEN-BELSEN:
THE FIRST KISS

We all grow up among the dead.
But for a child, you had so many.
In fifteen minutes—less time than it took
to kill hundreds—you could ride

your white, three-speed bicycle, out
through the front gate, over the cricket pitch,
down past the pig farm and into
Bergen-Belsen. The house you grew up in

appears on a postcard mailed
by soldiers of the Wehrmacht to their families
sometime during their training
in nineteen thirty-nine; contained,

toward the end of the war, 869 Gypsies,
Jews, and others—overflow from the camp
next door as Stalin advanced and Hitler
panicked and prisoners were shuffled west.

It was here you had your first kiss—
in an attic room and under curfew
while the military police and a knot
of squaddies home from manoeuvres

invaded the gardens and neighbourhoods to shoot
rabid dogs and foxes. What did you know
about tenderness: you kissed him so hard,
leaning in, your lips like a railing,

and you refused the wet drawbridge of his tongue;
and there you were, cantilevered

across the abyss two bodies become
when they are touching. And behind your lips,

the fender of your teeth and your tongue
dreaming in its grave. Because you felt no desire
you knew there was nothing
worth closing your eyes for and so you gazed

beyond him, through the window,
at the crushing loneliness of summer, the engine
of each leaf busy with its visions, and the light,
preoccupied, turning its back: bright

acoustics of the world's indifference.
The shooting party worked without talking,
but you heard them pass—the lave
and the backwash of their footfalls catching

beneath the summer's wide brim of leaves—
but all you could think of were dogs
and foxes, their mouths full of damage, running,
frenzied, through fields and gardens with a sheath

of madness on every tooth; of the sweet
and clever hearts of men scuttled by killing;
and then everything began to unravel: the boy
you were kissing became dangerous because

he was a boy and might well grow up
to be a man schooled in murder, like those outside;
like the guards and the Kommandants of Bergen-Belsen,
who had once been boys;

who had all been fathers. The belief
in her father's goodness is a girl's last bastion
against the world. And with this gone, what hope
was there for you? The bird bones of happiness

went into exile. Your life became so small.
You pulled your hair out strand by strand,
you grew afraid of mirrors. Terrified
to leave your room after dark you pissed

under the carpet. Even your toys became dangerous.
Death, insistent as a jewel, was inside everything.
And, as easily as this, you lost your childhood.
And with that gone, what was left?

Bodies so still they were hurtful to watch.
Mouths useless as money.
Afterburn of panic, and graves in which thousands
traded their bones. Grass, willing and wild,

over such graves. Nostalgia for a child
who once believed in benevolence; whose body
had once lived like an animal, had felt
the world's terminal clasp and taken it,

happily, everywhere; a child
who would of course grow up and learn to kiss
with such finesse and tenderness that men
would never guess just how far in she was haunted.

THE LOVER

He takes the seat next to mine on the overnight
flight to Chicago, holding a single rose in a plastic,
leak-proof vial. He's in uniform and I see
he's been weeping. But it's not what I think.
Yes, he's on his way to meet a woman,
but a stranger, simply because she believes him to be
the person her lover spoke with as he lay dying.

He has nightmares, he says, and walks
backward in his sleep, trying hard to rewind
into the life he had before this one: to himself
as a boy with a jar of fireflies; to the calf
he raised that grew into a bull that slept
every night of its life under his window, the great
wedge of its head, its nose like a polished boot toe.

He feels like a thief, he says; as if he's taken from her
the one moment love prepares us for
all our lives. He wishes he had those proverbial
last words; that he could hand those final
moments to her, organized like a box of quality,
handmade chocolates with an insert
to inform her that the Heart is a Bitter-
sweet Truffle. But it wasn't like that.

There were no last words, just noise and the whole
street wavering and twenty yards ahead,
that man, her lover, lifting and literally
coming apart. Then fragments and pieces
and a coffin weighted so it felt and sounded
as if it held a complete man. He calls him
her lover, he says, because it gives his death

a mythical grandeur, but who can say
what her lover saw? The roil and the rubble
of the street as he was carried
upward? The shadow of his own body
dismantling? He has her lover's death speech
all prepared, he says, so it sounds a bit like Hamlet
dying in the arms of Horatio. Of course it's a lie,

he's never once seen a man actually die
like Hamlet. *But war is war,* he says, turning
to face me for the very first time,
and we are all so very tired of loss,
and we must, for each other,
build whole worlds out of what we lack.

THE CENTREFOLD

The semaphore of sleek flesh among the wrappers
and coffee cups, and at first I think there is something alive
among the garlands of rubbish. She is even the size
of a fetus or a small baby and I wonder
about the narratives that might lead backward
from this moment, about how she came to be
here, inside the bin of a public toilet,
at a rest stop, on the coast of North America.
She was once alive enough for the person
who placed her here: a woman, perhaps,
who felt diminished and hidden
on discovering her lover's secret stash
of magazines; who found herself driving
as far as her mood and the hour would allow
to dump the evidence; or a man, exhausted
and sick of his own addiction, a man
for whom a woman is always a fact
that must first become a fiction
before she can seem real to him. It's what
detectives do—create myths out of facts.
At least on television. And she does look
a bit like one of those bodies at a crime scene
that lie contorted in a puddled,
rubbish-strewn alley or flung against the dark,
mottled background of a forest floor with a few
cunningly placed leaves and scraps of fabric. I know
why no one burned her: such gestures have a most
terrible history. Bodies going into the fire.
I look at her, redolent there among the dated
papers, a worn wiper blade flung down

across her torso, and find myself wishing that I
could discard my body like this, toss it
without regret into a bin at a rest stop or a train station,
leave it in the dust by a fruit stand in a foreign country.
The body has always been a problem. And she
has that smile: the one worn by every woman
on display ever since da Vinci painted his Mona—
how to use the mouth itself as a promise
of entrance into the kingdom that lies
beyond the gates of the physical world;
and I think of that photo in last week's paper—
the one of the beautiful gunner crouching
down behind the shield of his armoured machine gun
who had a picture of his wife or his lover
stuck to the plating just over his right shoulder:
his woman, smiling and demure
as a Russian icon; his woman, on display
in the line of fire, but inviolate,
beyond harm, her smile a blessing falling
equally on all things as he
hoses the civilian neighbourhood with bullets.
And here we are, then: the soldier
and the soldier's lover, Mona Lisa and Leonardo,
that nameless, naked centrefold and me—all
of us held together for a moment in the pale
soak of sunlight coming through the fiberglass
roof of a public, unisex toilet until

I cover her up—her work, whatever we call it,
done; until I walk forward and the door
snaps shut behind me and there is the Pacific
with its bright, precise grammar of sails
and the wind peeled free from the water rattling

the sabres of the eucalypti; and here
is my lover, the man I have chosen, one
among millions, waiting, with his hands
in his pockets and his back to the wind. Alive
in this world. And still smiling.

INFIDELITY

After the first death there is no other.
      — Dylan Thomas

When the hawk slaked down into the garden and entered
the chittering bud of linnets and sparrows
feeding on the bread crumbs and stale cereal, you
were telling me the story of how
you took it upon yourself to bury, as you would
in the weeks to come most of your own platoon, the young
German—the first man you ever killed—
shot on the concrete forecourt of a textile
factory in Belgium. With a single bullet.
I need to believe you spent the war
safe from yourself, in reserve, your rifle
clean and unfired. But the tautness
of his skin dropped away like a sail losing the wind and the wet
purse of his mouth fell slack and eased open
to reveal its neat, stained wreaths of change.
After the first death there were many others and they all
rose up through this one. Out in the garden the hawk
rowed up from the earth with its burden leaving
a panic the colour of ashes and bone.
A slim warmth was trapped in the fabric
of his battle dress; there were twigs and feathers
of grass in his hair, and, as you dragged him, the dark
palm of the earth snagged him by the heels
and eased his boots off. But you were tired
and the grave so shallow and small his knees
rose up through the dirt. To shovel soil
across his face, you said, dead as he was, to throw
dirt into the gape of his mouth and over

63

the pale noose of each iris was an act
of infidelity against your own humanity
far worse than squeezing the trigger. That night
laid out beneath the empty looms of the factory
you dreamt of that grave at the edge
of the wood from which the knees of a dead man
rose like breasts through the dirt and at dawn
were ravenous for a woman. Not sex,
but the easy kindness that stands in attendance
whenever women are present. *You are married,*
you said, *to the first man you ever kill,* and then
you went outside to gather even the smallest
feathers that had drifted and caught
against the hedge. Still, after sixty years,
the terrible competency of your hands. You spaced
those small feathers widely like seeds in the soil
and were down on your knees so long the mist
and the sea fret stashed their silver among the fine hairs
of your jacket. A man, however well he lives, never lives
well enough to justify the harm he commits
with his own hands: *he bent at the knees so slowly,* you said,
then folded forward gently, with a sigh, like a woman's dress.

How to Use a Field Guide

That knife was honed and bright as a grass blade.
It fit neatly inside its own tight slot among other
knives in a wooden block on the counter.

I was sixteen, studying Shakespeare. I knew
about the unconscious and had read
all about Lady Macbeth washing her hands in air.

But when I discovered, low on the blade
and close to the handle, a red
blemish tempered into the metal, I saw

not evidence of past atrocities, but a portent
of butcheries still to come: some coded
instruction an intruder would recognize. So,

at night, and in secret, I began scrubbing
the tarnished blade of my mother's favourite knife.
Summer in England. Every day I took my guide

to the butterflies of Britain and Northern Ireland,
and wove through the churchyard and on
past Wildblood's Rendering where ears and bones

and hooves arrived each day from the slaughterhouses
in lidless bins and barrels, and so
down to the fields by the river and into

that long, moist lung of air in which all rivers run.
Sometimes, I found an ear forgotten in the gutter.
The men who worked there, I noticed them,

too, and believed that working with the dead
must teach them something important
about tenderness. They were large,

bright lures in their slick, yellow aprons, and lust
was the world's dark commerce my flesh
walked into without permission. So

it began: every night Wildblood's men
broke into my dreams, and just as in every epic
and every myth where the sword finds its way

into the hero's fist, that knife unsheathed
itself from its deep wooden pocket. Every
night they pried my shirt buttons open

with the tip of the blade and sliced through
the elastic waistband of my underwear
and made love to me, right there,

on the shag-pile carpet, their deep mouths
ransacking my mouth. I became a child
afraid of dreaming and would hide that knife

in a drawer at night beneath the ladles
and the plastic spatulas and leaf
through my guide to the butterflies of Britain

and Northern Ireland because each new page
was a new landscape into which the butterflies
that lived there had been painted; because,

page by page, I could work myself
into that world: Peacock, Comma, Common Blue,
Ringlet, Swallowtail, Meadow Brown. Look:

a Gatekeeper trolling the hems and the verges
of a field and, in that field, a fox in his suit of fire
crossing the open ground between two copses.

Look: on the forest's border, the slim flag
of the Wood White feeding on the bellflowers
and harebells; through trees, between dark trunks,

a sunlit clearing like a necklace of green beads.
In the picture I loved best of all, a rare
White Admiral was resting on the emerald

slap of a leaf, a remnant of paradise waiting
to be claimed; beyond, a field so flawless I knew
its green could open no further out of itself.

And no clouds anywhere because, as any
fool knows, clouds make paradise feel less hopeful.
And there, in the distance, a small herd

of Jerseys who would escape every possible future
but this one: a late afternoon, bright with nostalgia—
the world as it was before the body

had been presented to itself as a problem—where,
in a fritter of sunlight beneath the canopy of a single
oak, they wait, untroubled, for the evening milker.

DOWNY WOODPECKER

It took three days but she drilled
through the shingles and into the wooden
frame of the house. I liked the sounds
of her coming and going, like voices
heard in childhood from another room.
If this were my house I'd let her stay
so that when she slept I would be sleeping,
close by, through the wall. But this is not
my house and so under duress I cover
her entrance over and am ransacked
by the way she flies bemused from the house
to the tree limb, from the tree limb
to the house all afternoon. I'm sorry,
I say. I'm sorry. All that effort.
That honest, pure work. I imagine
she feels like I do after waking from a dream
so real I am certain that the world
I have invented for myself exists.
Then the bewilderment and the panic
and the barge of the body scuttled by grief.
This is my poverty: to live in a house
from which I have to turn the small gods
of the world away. And then to watch them
turn away, which they do, without rancour.

Dinner in the Suburbs

Spring, and a cardinal drops his three-pronged
call, bright and precise like new pins,
and the daylight slips a little, like a letter, into
the envelope of evening. Easy figures: something
to go with the six o'clock news, and that wide
pre-dinner bonhomie a strong martini brings in
on its arm like a Hollywood starlet. The world
has changed so little. War is rootless still, slipping
over borders without passport or papers, and even
with the sound turned down, objects on the outskirts
and fringes of footage still tell stories.
A wrecked bike in the rubble once the dust
has settled. A suitcase left by a bench in the park.
Spent bullets on the road's wide shoulder and the dying
and the starving of today are the starving
and the dying of Biafra and Vietnam;
of thirty-five years ago. The year you turned ten.
The year Armstrong and Aldrin left their boot prints
on the moon. Those who suffer, you were told
as a child, are closer to god, even though
the starving and the dying never do seem close
to god; even though terror can look like rapture
in the way that it drives us out from the garden
of the body, unwilling to witness what, if anything,
will be left when everything is over. *If there is*
no god, you think, pouring a second martini, savouring
the oily wash of gin then turning to your plate
with its scaffold of ribs and its small,
overcooked logjam of green beans, *then the problem*
of how to get closer to him is solved. How easy,

even for a god, to turn away from the world.
Slight pressure on the right button
and the screen goes dark. Outside along the street
porch light after porch light flickers on as a lone raccoon
trips sensor after sensor on its rounds. And the day,
a treaty written up to be broken, signed and sealed.

AFTER WATCHING TELEVISION
I STEP OUTSIDE

away from facts, into
the indecisions of half-darkness because I
have just seen the survivors of Beslan weeping
and repeating the story of how the hostaged children
began eating their flowers, passing
along petals to those who had none. From his post
in the black oak the horned owl swings the calm
disc of his face toward me. And who
started it? Whose heart opened first, like a hand?
Whose hand a dish of petals? The flesh
would not survive long on gifts such as this, but the spirit
could sustain itself forever.
We could say that the children taking off their clothes
in the heat were flowers stripped of their petals,
except there are moments we must refuse
to trade for metaphor. Even if the world is a fiction,
some facts are literal. Fact: the children ate their flowers.
Fact: those with flowers shared them with those
who had none. Which version do you prefer:
the one in which each flower is eaten
down to its very last petal; or the one in which a few
petals are lost, knocked out of hands
and scattered, so that the women and the men
wandering later in the rubble discovered the heart's
wafer-thin, bright sustenance among the wreckage?
Both stories end the same way. Fact: *We stumbled,*
they said, *through the wreckage,*
over guts and body parts. God, forgive us,
they said, *we could not help them.* A sudden flush
of movement in the small harbours of the body
where grief gathers. It is dark now.
The long, slow bloom of an owl's call deep in the wood.

FOUR GIRLS

on the overpass in bikinis, caught
behind the net of the chain-link fence,
and I'm wondering whose idea it really was
to stand there virtually naked and wave
at and catch the traffic coming both ways.
I doubt they are even aware of the bikini's
tragic history—how Reard insisted
he'd named it for the island, not
the bomb blast, but then admitted
he was cashing in on a hot topic, even so.
But this is history and it's not fashionable,
especially when you're young
and virtually naked with so many men
moving beneath you. These are girls
who have recently discovered
that the bodies they have are the bodies
men want more than they
themselves do. And such beauty in itself
is not dangerous but it puts them at risk
as they flirt and turn like the spinners
and spoons my father taught me to use
to lure the perch and the pike up
into daylight and air. That's what I was
as a girl—a quiet magician, casting beguilement
and false promise over the water. And the one
lure believed by many to be
the most devastating was my favourite—
the Syclops with its life-like, side-to-side waggle,
multi-flash and vibration, with its wire
strand soft as boot lace—springy, with no memory.

Who could fail to love the head of a fish
ripping like an axe head through the skin
of the water. And all these men moving
under them in sports cars and hatchbacks and suburban
utility vehicles are wearing even
the promise of their large hands like expensive
accessories. This is what they imagine,
these girls: hands that will reel them in,
unfasten them and have them raking for air. And then
spill them back into the wet
coffin of their lives. They will learn to confuse
sex with salvation. I've done it, too. All my life.
And it's made me lonely. It's history
and it's not fashionable, but before they were born
Bikini was removed forever, vapourized
by Bravo in nineteen fifty-four. And while
the islanders of the atoll still remain homeless,
marooned on a distant island with no reef
and no lagoon when in the past they'd sailed
their canoes as far as the eye could see,
these four girls in scraps of fabric named
for a literal hot topic are spinning slowly
above a slick, wide spine of traffic. Glanced at.
Desired. Forgotten. And I'm pressing on
in second, sliding through the belt of shadow
under the overpass. Remember, a lure

is crafted to respond to every
eddy and swirl in a current. In my mirror the girls
are slim silhouettes. And how small they become.
How precious and precise. Out of their depth.

SKYLARKS

Within the slim purse of pure silence
after the barrage and before
the whistles sent the first wave over the top,

they heard skylarks singing. In real life
such things rarely happen: such marriages of violence
and small mercies. But the men in the trenches

knew exactly where they were. It took
only a moment—the skylarks
singing and rising and rows of faces

pivoting skyward and then madness, bitterness, man
after man boosting the man before him up
the ladder where their bodies blew open, throwing

themselves everywhere like dark mist or dust.
The mold that bloomed on everything.
The body's priceless rubble.

The terror and sheer bad luck of a man
pinned down in no-man's-land, where,
as the dead cooled down, their lice, moving house,

became his, proving how generous
the dead can be. Rattle and witter of gunfire.
In the shattered fields skylarks flustered back into song.

In the dugouts, the masturbating and the weeping
that followed. *Choose,* says history, as if
there is ever any difference

between the weeping and the singing.

LOOKING AT PHOTOGRAPHS,
IMPERIAL WAR MUSEUM, LONDON

It's their hands I notice first—fingers
cradling the stock of a rifle, unfolding
a field map or feeding bandoliers
into the breech of a Vickers machine gun; fingers
on the rim of a helmet raised in greeting; the hands
of a whole battalion raising their helmets in greeting
on their way to the Somme front line in 1916.
But it's hands not occupied, for the moment, with war
that move me most—hands lost in pockets, cheating
at cards, lighting cigarettes. Long-fingered,
dirty, competent—some with the bright lasso
of a wedding ring, but most without. Hands
writing letters. May 17, 1917, and someone
is sending a message by pigeon from a trench
on the Western Front, and what the camera
has given us is that moment right after
the moment when the young signalman unlocked
the soft prison of his fingers
to fling the bird skyward. The truth the eye
misses, the heart never fails
to recognize, and this is not simply
one more document of history or one more
fragment of war: this is a man
standing, empty-handed,
forever. Look at the pale cradle he has made
of his fingers; think how much it could hold.
And these are the hands that would slit
a man's throat if they had to, and yet
I know the magic the hands of a man can work
on the body of a woman he loves. There is evidence

everywhere—murder and beauty. The bird's
wings are blurred like swirling
shrouds, like vestments, like skirts and the man's
arms are caught in the follow-through—easy, natural,
a gesture like the green-smooth follow-through of spring;
and his body, too, beginning to rise.

THE FIRST SUNDAY OF HUNTING SEASON

*Hunting season. Busy nude clubs in MN and ND looking for
good girls to make big $$. Hunting season is here! No experience
necessary.*

— employment notice in a Minneapolis weekly

The men are out in their orange cuirasses.
The good girls are rehearsing their moves. In the pews
of the churches in small towns are women,
with their eyes on their prayer books, the flurry

of pages like a snicker of ash. To kill, we are told,
is a boy's rite of passage (though into what
new terrain I never could fathom because I
loved a soldier once who was lost forever

inside the country of his own body); but it's why,
at this moment, there are men and boys
perched in blinds, discussing the nuances
of firearms. Poets, of course, butcher

nothing but their own ideas: the words on the page
are the duff and the epitaph of an impulse
in its first perfect stirrings. So, bless the shoulders
we lean against such language; and the heart's

four neighbourhoods, its exclusive, gated communities:
bless them. Bless the deer that slide, over and over,
out of the hunter's sights and saunter, out
of common sense or instinct, onto private land

and so flaunt themselves in the open all season long.
And bless the good girls from Minnesota and North Dakota
dancing naked after dark for men their fathers' age, men
who return to their motels and their campers

with a loneliness nothing in this life will kill.
Bless the boy so bewitched by the black
ink pots of a deer's hooves that he cannot fire his rifle.
Bless the bullet that jams in the chamber.
Bless the grave of every poem.

From the Mouth to the Source

It drills right through him, the force
spinning him around so that he dances
a full pirouette as it enters his left breast
just above the nipple. A veteran
after six weeks of war,
you can put five shots inside a four-
inch circle from two hundred yards.
Muzzle velocity: two thousand,
four hundred and forty feet per second.
Chamber pressure: nineteen point five
tons per square inch. He was fifty
yards away and all it took
was this one bullet that was shipped
across the Channel, trucked to the front
from a port in France and loaded,
just that morning, from its stripper clip
and then cradled all day in the chamber
of your rifle. Before you recover
from the recoil he is on his back and it's cold
enough to see the reach of his breathing, forced
from his mouth in great streamers, growing
shorter and shorter as he settles
himself deeper into the dirt: you feel it—
like someone sitting down on the edge
of a bed when you are sleeping. It feels
real the way death in a dream feels real and then
in daylight, when you wake, more real still.
Then, in profile, the slack, easy hollow
of his open mouth like a beggar's bowl;
and you, for now, with everything

still left to give and across the Channel
the girl who worked on the bullet has finished
her shift at the factory and just now walked
through the door of her tiny flat in Coventry.
Nightfall. You and your platoon
are out of your slits, on the move; the girl
in Coventry pulls her curtains, puts bread on the table,
and butter, and jam if she's lucky. She's too tired
to bathe. And the dead German soldier a small
part of the darkness, now, between you.

THE MAP

Pile the bodies high at Austerlitz and Waterloo.
Shovel them under and let me work—
I am the grass; I cover all.

And pile them high at Gettysburg
And pile them high at Ypres and Verdun.
Shovel them under and let me work.
                                          — Carl Sandburg

Your father's dead will not leave you in peace.

Last night in a dream you were back
on that corner in Xanten where Jenkins the medic
took a bullet in the neck and your father went down
on his knees and saw the animal
behind a man's eyes breaking its cage and departing;
and Sergeant Rogers, his hands blown off
by his own grenade, was there, tottering
through the rubble and pleading with you to please
open his fly so he could take a piss. And Grant,
of course, in pieces, a soft jigsaw of blood and flesh.
And when you woke you were thinking of Antony
weeping over the ransacked body of Caesar and claiming

Thou art the ruins of the noblest man . . .
And these were your father's men—people
your father could name. The body, your father
is telling you over his shoulder as you follow
his light-blue jacket along the track on the bank
to the place he's had marked in memory for sixty years,
was nothing, nothing: just a word to describe

what it felt like to know the world was lost to him
already. And what relief it must have been, then,
to leave battle behind for a while and discover
the permanence of his own flesh when, in its loneliness,
he placed it down beside someone else's loneliness.
And slept. Smell of brine

and fast-moving water, the whine of a car in the distance
climbing up through its gears. And your father
in his brown, wide-fit shoes, with a shine at the knees
of his trousers as if he has knelt, every day, for years,
in prayer. This is how history haunts those
who survive it: yesterday you were walking the streets
of Xanten; and tomorrow you will drive to the warehouse
in Alpon where your father, after calmly questioning
a direct order, stayed awake to watch a full moon lowered
like a host into the lake. And today you are standing

on the bank of a river, on the exact
square of earth where your father was shot.
It's so peaceful, you say, without thinking. Because
there are tiers of cloud right down
to the horizon and in the flooded ditches
the marsh flowers have all at once
fallen open. *It was the peace,* he says,

*I hated most of all: those times when it was so
quiet and still you'd hear the chill, passive click
of a bayonet being fixed.* In a field to your left,
the sound of hooves kissing stone, then a cow's long
sigh like a moist room. To have come so far.

To have waited so long. To find nothing under your feet
but the grass, doing its work. To glance back
as you are leaving and see the depressions your shoes
have made in the grass and realize you were standing so close
that your bodies must have been touching.

LOVE AND THE HANGMAN IN CROATIA

Every morning and evening on the balcony
we play Hangman. The words, we agree, have to be
in Serbo-Croatian: it is a way, we decide,
to learn the language and so feel less
like tourists. Out beyond the harbour,

threads of surf where the ocean stands
against the shore plucking its sleeves;
and the fishermen, who have been out
since dawn, have left their boats roped
along the pier and come up from the quayside

with their donkeys, fish piled in their panniers
like embroidered slippers. We watch them cross
the wooden bridge over the narrow stream, the hooves
of the donkeys like lacquered ornaments, the plush
gutter of each ear nodding freely

like heavy blossom. I tell you I believe
that the way we assemble the hanged man
has meaning. Because the body is a metaphor.
And what we do to the body is a metaphor.
You build your body backwards, adding

the scaffold of the gallows as if
it were an afterthought, an accessory,
like a Homburg or a handbag, and your
last gesture is always to connect that tiny
length of rope to the neck. But I build my

gallows before anything else. The rope drops, then
comes the head round as a button; then
the banner of the body. And the legs, always akimbo,
even though in real life they would hang straight
down, and inside the long, slack bell of each pant leg

would swing the femur's thin clapper. I add
the right arm last of all because this is the arm
that owns the hand which moves the pencil
over the paper. In the evening, when the fishermen
return, there is always one among them

who has shouldered the empty panniers, let
the tether drop and is walking with his free hand resting
on the withers of his tired companion. Shadows
of clouds and birds. In the centre of the table
like tiny urns, clay jars of jam and honey. We come up

with *patnja* and *klaonica* and *razaranje* easily
enough, and the words assemble, letter by letter,
into their assigned spaces on the paper—those dashes
like a run of stitching, like a missile's trajectory
in a child's drawing of war—as into our small cups we pour

one more black bullet of coffee.

On the Train to Leningrad
with Osip Mandelstam

For life, you wrote; *for life . . . I'll give up everything.*
And I fell in love with passion disguised as necessity

and when we stopped at Ostashkovo I knew
I was in trouble already. It was the tightly-
buckled belt and the Cossack flare
of his greatcoat; the perfect, assertive tenor
of his boots on the stones of the platform.

He brought the cold in with him. He wore
a leather glove on the hand he held out
for my papers. The hand that had been trained
to pull the trigger was bare.

Within his voice, stones churning
inside a river's tight throat. I remember wondering
if a man with so much moisture in his mouth
would be a good lover. And what could I do
but hand my papers over and watch his tongue
flicker like a fish. It was the first time

I had ever looked a rifle straight
in its black eye.

Outside, sunlight clicking between trees;
a river, and across the river in a field
a black horse, dozing, as if every unhappiness
it had ever known had slipped down
the long bones of its legs and vanished
into the small pool of its own shadow.
It was nineteen eighty and Europe was a dream

with a divided soul and I had been living,
remember, for weeks among your people
and I was far from home and lonely
and suddenly hungry and that soldier
at the station in Ostashkovo? That man

was like a country ready for ruin, and I
would have willingly given up everything
for a taste of him. *Careful,* I heard you saying:
be careful. You must be careful and cautious
about passion. Even Stalin, remember,
had passion. To be forced to speak out
against your own heart is death. To stay silent
is death. You refused to do either,
and it was death. And in the book I was reading
the words of your life were in translation
but the world they made
would never be destroyed by language. Yes,

even Stalin had passion:
He rolls the executions on his tongue like berries.
And these were your words, and they sent you

into exile, and all I could think of was Nadezhda
committing your poems to memory, the salt
from the executioner's hands already
on the handle of the axe.

CAROLINA GRASSHOPPERS

In secondary school, in biology, in order to help us memorize the
characteristics of living things, we were given the mnemonic
GRIMNER: Growth, Respiration, Irritability, Movement,
Nutrition, Excretion and Reproduction. This was The Word for the
facts, for observable things. It said absolutely nothing about what it
felt like to be alive.

— Journal entry

Mr. Davis gave us The Word, placing
beside each one of us a spiral-bound, splash-proof
guide to dissection and our own
special-order Carolina grasshopper
submerged underwater in a chipped, high-sided dish
because, underwater, its strong legs anchored
in wax, it was easy
to seduce even that golden body open.
It took almost no effort to sever that knot
of muscle, release the forewing and set it adrift
like a beautiful, lost oar; and even less to tease
out a hind wing and marvel at its burning
hem of yellow and how it would have folded,
fan-like, against the body when not in use. Imagine
having wings and choosing not to use them.
That year, reading Whitman, I came to believe
in desire as a state of grace—the promise
of terminal happiness—and went on to test
this belief in a windbreak of trees beyond
the playing field where we were sent, in mixed
pairs, to kneel over two square feet of earth
and undergrowth and pass the whole afternoon
counting and naming. The body is impossible

to account for, and if it all comes down to a single
word then let it be something worthy, a match
for what I discovered in a windbreak
with a boy who turned the dark purse
of my body inside out, who was all
muscle and imperative, who would later enlist
and die, facedown, in the wet heath of the Falklands.
Who, I want to believe, had time to remember
the way he and I lay down and the rise
of his own excitement at the slight resistance
of his buttons and the small squeak
as the last one finally released and my wet mouth
hovered carefully over his nipples, the sudden rattle
of breath as some part of him broke free.
That it was April, so the new and unused
lips of the blooms had parted, but only
just. I remember the way his eyes never closed
completely as we did whatever it was

that passed for sex: that slit
of brightness beneath his lashes—just a glint—
as if some small insect had decided, suddenly, to open
its wings toward the myth of another world.

The Good Doctor in Nagasaki

for Gunther von Hagens

What makes us move? Who makes us move?
                    Who created this misfortune?

It's the muscles that fascinate me.
                    The most impressive thing I saw:
                    very young girls, their skins peeled off.

There must be a god.
                    I look across far and wide,
                    where is the Lord?

What's amazing is that it's an actual
human body. It looks like jerky.
                    From palms joined in prayer
                    my parents
                    charred black keep slipping.

Did you see the one where the nerves
are just dangling?
                    Those alive died in pain, one by one.

Don't bang on the glass!
                    Behold, this is the inferno!

This one's missing his testicles.
                    Her hair was burning.

Momma, I really want to leave now.
                    Mother didn't come, no matter
                    how long we waited.

Don't you wonder what their dreams and hopes were?
                Whether or not I listen
                ghosts sob on the atomic field.

I wonder what this one did for a living.
                Dragonfly,
                I pick up wood to burn the children.

Will you look at that! The brain
is just a basket of blood vessels.
                Near the hypocenter blooms in dust
                a red heavenflower.

Can you name something that would kill
your brain cells?
                It is hard to die by my own hand.

Uncle Jeff makes an incision right here
and replaces that joint with a metal one.
                We built a house of zinc sheets in the ruins.

There's a pregnant woman over there and you can see
the dead baby inside her.
                I lay her dead body on the roadside.
                Night dawns early.

I'm not sure I agree with what's going on here.
                A single bird hurtles, splitting the blue sky.

You could sit here all day, just looking,
and still have no answers.
                In the Cathedral, in the ruins of boundless expanse,
                I stayed one night criticizing God.

This one's called "Lady of Arteries and Bones."
It sounds religious.
>   Mother became bones before my eyes.

How moving it is that they still have all their eyelashes.
>   She fell crumbling between the embers.

You could gnaw on those bones.
>   Bones like flower petals.

This is so beautiful I can't describe it.
>   Flowering buckwheat a single stalk for a grave
>   we have survived.

What holds it all together?
>   Picking up the ant on my palm
>   I put it back on the bombed land.

GROWING UP IN BERGEN-BELSEN:
SLEEPING WITH ANNE FRANK

We all grow up among the dead.
But for a child, I had so many. In fifteen

minutes—less time than it took to kill hundreds—
I could ride my white, three-speed

bicycle, out through the front gate, over
the cricket pitch, down past the pig farm and into

Bergen-Belsen. I saw the tangled
bones of the dead in everything: in the pin-

glitter of blown rain and how the wind
chewed the marsh grasses into snarls; even

in the way my brother and his new love
laced their fingers. Grisaille of branches

in the half-dark of dawn and dusk. Crumble
of new light inside the river's pocket. Anne

Frank was there already when I arrived
and by then her bones had lived longer

beneath the grass than above it. It happens.
And bones forget even themselves.

It was spring and I was tired of spring,
of its pushings and shovings;

of shoots like slick bullets and the cherry
bleeding out along its branches, because,

eventually, even this gets used up: behind
the greenness and the heat, the slow slide

out again, and, eventually, the lulls
between a bird's songs lengthen. Then become

omissions. Like a place not set at table.
Then darkness unlike any other. And I was tired

of the boys I knew who nailed newts
and snakes to the trunks of trees just to see

how they would die. I used to wonder
what possible difference it could make

how we died. But it does, it does. And to possess a body
is to be possessed by terror, and there were times

when I would rather lie down with the dead
than be lost among the living and I would place my lips

against the grass and speak, as rain speaks, down
the green corridor of every blade: *Anne,*

I whispered, *where are you now,* thinking
it strange how she had gone, so quickly,

from being pinned inside that prison
in Amsterdam to swinging, slowly,

through acres of dirt. Over the years
I put my forehead to the forehead

of each of the dead in turn, each fortress
of bone, and left nothing but the bruised

depression of my small body in the grass—a shadow
between two selves, where the grass, hurt open,

turned blue. I slept there often, the sweat
of the grass everywhere in my mouth. This first hunger

has been my only hunger. It will be my last.

The Insect Collector's Demise

On mornings free of cloud, the insects
mistake my windows for clean platters
of sky and knock against them, seeking entry.

Some make hardly a sound—a sand grain
blown against glass; but others—butterflies,
for instance, kiss a bit harder and leave behind

a whiplash of dust. The mind is a jailer
whose job it is to wake us
when we are not sleeping and I

am suddenly the child I used
to be, running amuck through the garden
with my killing jars and my nets; a child

so in love with the world that she carried
pieces of it everywhere so she would never forget.
There was nothing beautiful

in such dying, in such bluster and panic. My net
had a mesh as soft as a stocking and it held
the scent of chemicals and breakage—a bitterness

like tarnished metal. Every day
there were items left behind—torn wings
like scraps of propaganda, the leg

of a cricket like a dropped hat pin. Forget
formaldehyde and ethyl acetate, forget
the suspect, precarious terrains

into which all collectors go
for a rare specimen; imagine what happens
to a child in that moment

when the matte-black pin, thin as a horse hair,
breaches a cricket's lacquered façade and passes
smoothly, and without resistance, through

the body beneath. In the killing jar,
the crickets were the worst of all—their leaps
against the glass the music

of someone fiddling with the small change
in his pocket. What hubris
to think the insects loved their lives

any less than I loved mine. Each one
a verb snatched from the world's mouth.
This is how I grew afraid of details, of all

the precisions of suffering and fell in love
with landscapes viewed from a distance, where
it was everything I could not see

that saved me; where, if there were animals
they were small and clean on the earth's
green manicure: sunlight washing like varnish

over the backs of black cattle in the fields; sheep
falling to their knees to get closer
to the sweetest, lower stems of the grass.

And being rewarded. From a distance
each tree was a green trawl of light.
Too far away to hear the leaves' sad

fricative or every tiny murder
in the dirt, this was a world
in which even the hooves and the teeth

of the horses grazing under the eaves of an oak
had never once hurt the grasses; there were
no blast zones of pewter feathers,

no flusters of corruption or scandal
on the leaves' plain crockery;
no ticks dug in between the jackdaw's

feathers, not a single moth like a banner
in the jaws of an ant. Not a single ant
in a blackbird's beak. At the end

of every trouble, I thought, were fields
like this, fields like sunlit platforms.
God's failed attempts at imagining paradise.

It was everywhere I wasn't: I could step
right into it and never arrive;
it was always behind me, where the grass

had already shrugged off
the dark kiss of my small boots.
And before me the wrestle of the river,

all purpose and no wastage, and I could feel
the trout's perfect fit within it
where the current grew snug on the inside curve.

    I have wasted my life trying to enter this promise.
    I will waste whatever life I have left.
    In the inch-deep darkness of a tree's body, the egg

    of the ichneumon, that persuasive burglar, lies
    next to the egg of the wood wasp.
    What the world gives, the world

then takes away.

ROAD KILL

What makes the engine go?
Desire, desire, desire.
　　　— Stanley Kunitz

My first lessons in what it meant to have a body were nothing
sexual, even though they had everything to do
with hunger. (Think of Eve
in her cravings for knowledge eating the world
and losing everything.) I

would not stop browsing through death's
extensive wardrobes and began to feel cheated
by those that remained unopened even after
they'd been kissed with such force that lariats
and loops of intestine broke loose and spilled
out of their mouths. Finding them at dawn

was best, as if they had broken
through from Eden—through the door I
fell asleep to find—and had slipped, somehow,
off night's black decks. I had my favourite:

the crow cemented to the road, its wings
from tip to shoulder loose and lifting
on the draft as we went past. In half-sleep
I'd often felt my own hands flitter like this. Weight
of the body. Weight of death. What difference?
The dead were specific and singular

and possessing a body
meant certain loneliness. I remember
the Peugeot in the road where it had stalled;
my mother lamenting and my father
turning away, his shirt smooth
across the width of his back;
and the doe, eyes closed, in her own
troubled suspension, a froth
of warning at her lips; blood and beneath
the blood a polished blink of intestine. And there
I was, reaching out to touch the pallium
of darker hair around the doe's thin shoulders
as her hooves fluttered and clattered
lightly together like dice. I thought the dead
would step out of their torn pockets
on the tarmac and come forward, like gods,
through their own absence; I thought the flesh

was a door but it was always a mirror, a pan-flash,
a wrung-out gleam, the afterburn of effort. Shattered
windbreak of ribs. Gullet's sleeve.
And how easy it was to overlook the heart's
plump slipper, there between the lungs' little kitbags.
But the dead were good to me; they graced

me with a new language, with *nacreous* and *viscera;*
taught me that the body is the only mouth

in which appetite rehearses its singing. This
hunger, I thought, was the soul in disguise and this
became the belief I began to inhabit, and this

belief became a problem: think of Eve
in her cravings for knowledge eating the world
and losing everything. I don't know

how a girl learns that it isn't polite
to give herself over, like an animal, to the oblivion
of appetite; that her displays of hunger
make others nervous. But I devised
new ways of looking—noticing the dead

on the road up ahead and positioning
my gaze so I could look, on reaching them,
without turning my head. And it's true:
if you disguise something well enough,
even you yourself can fail to recognize it.
A day came when I failed
to pinpoint the exact spot on the tarmac. And then,

a day when I stopped trying. The song pulled
its tongue from every grass blade. The lit runway
of every leaf went nowhere. My desire
became oblique. Later, I would look at men
this way, with a hunger clamouring
at the back of my throat where words should be.
Hive in a box. A craving
that had swallowed nothing
but itself for years and forgotten its own name.

ROPES

for Christoph

> *There is the one side and the other,*
> *and between there is the wall.*
> — Ken Smith

His rooms were all foliage and daylight
with fish tanks on the sill of every window
so that every single chair he had
offered a view of tetras and danios
patrolling and sewing their colours across
the city's skyline. But it wasn't

their colours he loved. There are times,
even in our own language, when every word
sounds foreign, but she loved the way his words
pulled up next to hers and meant
the same thing—*love, Liebe, meine*
Herzallerliebste. My beloved. In sex, language
gave each of them the same understanding

of desire, but his past, she knew, was a piece
of rubble the size of a die, chipped
from that corner near the Brandenburger Tor
and slipped, without fail, into the pocket
of whatever coat he wore because he had no choice
but to carry with him everywhere
the things he could not escape from.
Over his bed, a print of that famous
view looking east from the tower
on Bernauer Straße toward the block

of flats he'd lived in then; the church and the wall
so close he must have kicked it in his sleep.
In the foreground, on western soil, the viewing
scaffold's small, crude platform which he
couldn't help but see, every day, out of his window;
which she couldn't help but climb, on a field trip,
in her blue and yellow bell-bottomed pantsuit—
a thin, sad girl, jostling about among her friends
like a bright float until she sank
down, once again, to street level and someone
took her picture as she teetered, heel to toe,
arms out, like wings, for balance
along the tramlines until they vanished
under the wall. While light fell

equally everywhere. And weather
passed. And clouds and birds. Sometimes

leaves and seeds. He would sit, he said,
at the window: darkness falling; night birds.
The scream of a dog sniped by mistake,
or maybe not, by a guard. Dry
rubbing of wire in the wind and music drifting
from a nightclub somewhere over in the West.
And the best moment of all: house lights
and street lights both coming on, simultaneously,
on both sides of the border

which, years from now, will be merely
two pale lines of bricks set flush
with the streets and cobblestones of Berlin,
where she will happily spend
a whole spring afternoon in Potsdamer Platz

watching him stride, oblivious to everyone, back
and forth across it. They will stand
on one side and let their shadows fall

on the other and, even after so much time—even
after almost twenty years—he will weep
at just how effortless such crossings can be.
I always knew, he said, *that you were part of it—*

my adolescent conspiracy of beauty: the girls
in his dreams were always girls from the West
who distracted the guards at every watchtower and played
the ladders of their long hair down
over the wall—hair thick and useful
as the woven ropes of the tugboats
down on the Spree where his father
worked the night shifts. Those ropes

were so real he would haul himself upward
out of sleep only to wake and find himself hard
in his own hands. The first birds
knocking against daylight. These days
she makes sure that when he wakes he is hard
in the curl of her fist and, *yes,* she reassures him, *yes,*
my hair was long back then.

WOLVES

What is it we are saying
about ourselves when we fail
so many? I dream

that the wolves weave
down to us
off the hills and it's as if,
like a print, love is made over
and over in me. Saving

myself means keeping them
moving like fire
among the trees, breathing
me back into something
resembling my life. How much

I love this earth is answered,
here, where the wolves run
all day, sometimes

all night, oiled
and blazing
with their own hunger. They pass
like love

across something less
and more than distance, something

I might step out on and so walk
and walk and never come back.

Notes

The Bergen-Belsen poems

In 1933 the German army began building a training camp and several military ranges east of Bergen, near Hannover, in northern Germany. In spite of protests from the local populace, eleven villages were evacuated and the training camp became known as Hohne, after one of the evacuated villages. Bergen-Belsen was set up less than a mile to the south of Hohne.

Originally, Bergen-Belsen was a workers' camp erected for the labourers employed on the Hohne Camp and Ranges project. In 1940 it became a prisoner-of-war camp, first for French and Belgian soldiers, then, in 1941, after the Soviets joined the Allies, a Soviet prisoner-of-war camp known as Stalag XI-C. By the spring of 1942, 18,000 of the 20,000 Soviet prisoners of war had died of hunger, cold, and disease.

In 1943 a section of the camp was handed over to the SS, who established the "detention camp" Bergen-Belsen for Jews who were intended for exchange with Germans held in internment abroad. In 1944, Josef Kramer, previously at Auschwitz-Birkenau, became the new camp Kommandant.

In 1945, as the Soviet forces advanced, large numbers of prisoners were moved to Bergen-Belsen from camps in the east, and the SS took over part of Hohne Camp to house inmates as Bergen-Belsen became severely overcrowded. Several blocks in the southern section of Hohne Camp were wired off and surrounded with watchtowers: this became known as Bergen-Belsen Camp 2. The house I grew up in, named MB 85, was part of Bergen-Belsen Camp 2 and according to camp records housed over 800 Polish Jews, Gypsies, and "others."

The British liberated Bergen-Belsen on 15 April 1945, and Hohne Camp then became a hospital for the 60,000 people interred at Bergen-Belsen, which had officially been "designed" to hold 10,000 people. Hohne Camp was a home for Displaced Persons until 1950; after this, it became a NATO military base controlled by the British and the Dutch.

There were no gas chambers in Bergen-Belsen, since the mass executions took place in the camps further east. Nevertheless, in addition to the 18,000 Soviet prisoners of war, an estimated 50,000 Jews, Czechs, Poles, anti-Nazi Christians, homosexuals, and Gypsies died in the camp. Among them were the Czech painter and writer Josef Čapek, as well as Anne Frank and her sister Margot. The dead are buried in mass graves on the former concentration camp site, which is now an official Holocaust memorial.

"FOR THOSE HELD CAPTIVE FOR DECADES IN DARKNESS"
The lines quoted are from Walt Whitman's poem "The Return of the Heroes."

The Thiepval Memorial is the largest British war memorial in the world and commemorates the Anglo-French offensive on the Somme. It carries the names of over 73,000 British and South African men who have no known grave and who fell on the Somme between 1 July 1916 and 20 March 1918. Designed by Sir Edwin Lutyens, the memorial is 150 feet high and has sixteen piers on whose faces the names of the missing are inscribed. It stands on a concrete raft ten feet thick, submerged nineteen feet underground—the solution to building over the dugouts and tunnels that formed part of the German second line. It was unveiled on 31 July 1932. The Canadian missing of the Somme are commemorated on the Vimy Ridge Memorial, the Australians on the Villers Bretonneux Memorial, the Indians at Neuve Chapelle, the Newfoundlanders at Beaumont Hamel, and the New Zealanders at Longueval. It is estimated that the various Somme offensives claimed 195,000 French, 420,000 Commonwealth, and between 450,000 and 650,000 German casualties. Of the 58,000 British casualties on the first day alone (1 July 1916), almost 20,000 were killed in action or died from their wounds.

"SELLING HONEY ON THE ROAD TO SARAJEVO"
Sections in italics are found poems from *Hearts Grown Brutal: Sagas of Sarajevo* by Roger Cohen (New York: Random House, 1998).

"*ESPENBAUM* IN BERGEN-BELSEN, MAY 2007"
The first line of this poem is the first line of Paul Celan's poem *Espenbaum*. John Felstiner's translation of this line reads: "Aspen tree, your leaves glance white into the dark." *Selected Poems and Prose of Paul Celan*, trans. John Felstiner (New York: W.W. Norton, 2001). I found Celan's poem exactly as described: written out, in German, on a dead tree in Bergen-Belsen.

"LOVE AND THE HANGMAN IN CROATIA"
   patnja: pain, agony
   klaonica: shambles, slaughterhouse, butchery
   razaranje: holocaust, havoc, destruction

"On the Train to Leningrad with Osip Mandelstam"

Stanza 1: quote is from poem #127. Stanza 9: quote is from "The Stalin Epigram."

"The Good Doctor in Nagasaki"

Dr. Gunther von Hagens is a German anatomist and the inventor of plastination—a process he developed at the University of Heidelberg. This process makes it possible to lend rigidity to soft body parts (individual muscles, organs such as the lungs, or a single nerve, for example), and even specimens of the entire body can be stabilized and posed in such a way that they are capable of standing. The Body Worlds exhibit was at the Science Museum of Minnesota, St. Paul, in 2006, and this poem is a combination of overheard and found material. Lines left-justified are statements overheard at the St. Paul exhibit; indented lines are from memoirs, haiku, and tanka written by survivors of Nagasaki, from *The Atomic Bomb: Voices of Hiroshima and Nagasaki*, ed. Kyoko and Mark Selden (New York: East Gate, 1989). St. Paul and Nagasaki are sister cities. Coincidentally, this poem was completed on 4 July 2006—the day North Korea tested six nuclear missiles.

CPSIA information can be obtained
at www.ICGtesting.com
Printed in the USA
LVHW052052020321
680385LV00015B/514